THE FUNNY OLD BAG

When Joel's pet gerbil, Ernestine, had babies,
Joel gave one to his friend Valerie down the hall

THE FUNNY OLD BAG

By Lisl Weil

Parents' Magazine Press/New York

Copyright © 1974 by Lisl Weil
All rights reserved
Printed in the United States of America

Library of Congress Cataloging in Publication Data
Weil, Lisl.
　The funny old bag.
　SUMMARY: Big Howie gets his comeuppance at the same time the children finally find out what old Mr. Gugelhupf carries in his old black bag.
　[1. City and town life—Fiction] I. Title.
PZ7.W433Fu　[E]　73-13564
ISBN 0-8193-0717-3　　ISBN 0-8193-0718-1 (lib. bdg.)

and one to another neighbor.

Many children here at the housing project
would like to be Joel's friends.
Even Howie.
"Your next baby gerbil is mine," Howie said.
He made Joel promise, "Cross my heart
and hope to die."

Howie is big and he is strong.
At the drugstore he eats three Double Dips.

He *can*.

And when Howie acts funny, everyone laughs.
Of course Howie laughs the loudest.

Mr. and Mrs. Gugelhupf who live on the main floor only smile little smiles.

Even when Joel and Valerie say hello.

Old Mrs. Gugelhupf likes to feed the birds in the park. Also the squirrels.
Old Mr. Gugelhupf goes with her.

And he always carries a strange old black bag.
Such a funny looking bag it is!

"Old people walk funny," Howie said one day, walking just like the Gugelhupfs.

And all the children laughed.

"What do you think is in that old bag?" Joel asked.
"More birdseed and squirrel-nuts?" Valerie said.

"I know what!" said Howie. "It's a hot-water bottle to keep them warm because old people always shiver." Howie shivered.

But Joel could not stop thinking about that old bag.

So he asked his mama.

"Whatever it is, darling," she said,

"it is Mr. Gugelhupf's business. And we are not to pry into it." She gave Joel his goodnight kiss.

That night Joel dreamed
the old bag opened
and a fierce alligator
started to climb out.
The alligator got longer
and longer and closer
and then . . .
Luckily, Joel woke up.

It had been snowing all night, and now it was a fine day for playing in the park.

Mr. and Mrs. Gugelhupf were already busy feeding the hungry birds and squirrels.

To make a snowman is fun. To make the birds and squirrels scatter will be more fun, Howie thought. "Watch me!" He laughed.

He was running and he tripped.
His pants were torn and his leg was badly scraped.
"BOOH hoooh-ooooh!" Howie cried.

How loud he cried!
All the children ran to see what had happened.
Mr. and Mrs. Gugelhupf, too, came over as quickly as they could.

Mr. Gugelhupf took a look at Howie's leg.
"Don't worry," he said. "I'll fix it in no time."

And he opened his old bag. Joel held his breath.

What if an alligator should climb out now . . .

Inside the bag were many
small bottles and jars.
Mr. Gugelhupf picked one bottle.
"This is alcohol to clean your leg,"
he explained, putting some on a puff
of cotton.
With it he touched Howie's leg.
"BOOOH BOOOO HOOO-ooohoo!"
cried Howie, still louder.
Then Mr. Gugelhupf opened a round jar
with a salve in it.
"This will make your leg feel
just fine," he said.

After Mr. Gugelhupf had put a soft bandage around Howie's leg, Howie no longer hurt and he stopped crying. Mr. and Mrs. Gugelhupf helped Howie up.

"I used to be a doctor in my
younger years." Mr. Gugelhupf smiled.
And Mrs. Gugelhupf said, "Out of habit
he never goes anywhere without his doctor's bag."
Then she thought of something else.

"Come and let's have a party with cookies and some hot cocoa," Mrs. Gugelhupf said.

"Will you carry my bag?" Mr. Gugelhupf asked Joel.
And Joel very, very carefully carried the black bag.

While the children had cookies and hot cocoa, Mrs. Gugelhupf mended Howie's torn pants.

"Thank you, thank you," the children said,
when it was time to go home.

"Old people sure know how to do so-o many nice things," Joel said to Valerie. And because she is his best friend, he tells her his most important secrets. So he said, "I'm going to be a doctor

when I grow up. And the next time Ernestine has baby gerbils, I'm going to give one to Howie and then one to Dr. and Mrs. Gugelhupf!"

About the author-artist
As a child in Vienna, Austria, *Lisl Weil* loved music, dancing and drawing, and her parents encouraged her to develop her talents. When she came to America, she worked in all phases of art until discovering she liked doing children's books best of all. She makes her home in New York City where she also loves performing at the Young People's Concert Series, illustrating the music being played. She has been doing this for many years with the Little Orchestra Society at Philharmonic Hall, with other orchestras and on TV specials. She has illustrated over 70 books, about half of which she has also written—*Melissa, Shivers, The Wiggler,* etc. *Fat Ernest* (also a story about Joel and his gerbils) was her first book for Parents' Magazine Press.